D1175150

illustrated
chess for children

illustrated
chess for children

HARVEY KIDDER

Doubleday & Company, Inc.
Garden City, New York

ISBN: 0-385-05764-4 TRADE
0-385-05429-7 PREBOUND
Library of Congress Catalog Card Number 71-116220
Copyright © 1970 by Harvey Kidder
All Rights Reserved
Printed First in the United States of America
9   8

To my son, David —

"A liberally educated person is one whose mind works well in all areas."... Chess should certainly be part of his education.

Contents

Part One

What Is Chess?

Have you ever seen a chessboard? Wondered what it was all about?

Well, *that's what this book is all about—Chess—*the oldest and greatest skill game ever invented.

Imagine yourself *as a general, with an army to command!*

And the object of the game? *To capture the enemy Kings!*

Opposite you is another army and another general—and the better man will win! Exciting?

A chess army is much the same as our army today. It is made up of many types of soldiers and all types of people. Not all the soldiers in chess or in real life are professional military men. In fact most are amateurs, civilians, as we shall learn.

Just as people in real life are different, the pieces on the chessboard do not look alike nor do they all move in the same way. However, once we think of them *as real people,* we will always *remember how they move.*

DARIUS, THE FAMOUS PERSIAN KING

The game of chess was first played many centuries ago, in China, India, and Persia. In fact the name **chess** comes from the Persian *shah,* which means "king."

Later, Arab hordes (they were called Moors) overran Persia. They learned chess from the Persians, and brought the game with them when they invaded Spain.

From Spain chess quickly spread throughout all Europe.

This was about nine hundred years ago.

The Europeans gave the chess pieces the names we know today, which are **Castle, Knight, Bishop, King, Queen,** and **Pawn.**

They probably had trouble pronouncing and spelling the Persian names for the pieces, so they modernized the names to fit in with the way they lived.

Today they don't sound like very modern names but imagine for a moment that we were living six hundred years ago.

From a *castle* window we might very well see serfs or *pawns* working in the fields, perhaps a *knight* in his glittering armor approaching, or a *bishop* leaving a nearby church; and eventually the *king* and *queen* might appear somewhere on the scene.

No doubt in those days the names seemed as up-to-date and modern as they could possibly be — much the same as our speaking of the corner drugstore or the local policeman.

The six different chess pieces represent a complete cross section of medieval life. The way they look, *where they are placed* on the chessboard, the *way in which they move,* even their names, like the pieces of a puzzle, all relate to the picture we described above of medieval life with its pomp, pageantry and conflict.

And while this in itself is most interesting it is also most helpful as we learn the moves.

Now let us talk about the pieces, and who and what they stand for.

We start first with the **Pawns.** They are the serfs, the laborers, the poor. And as in any society there are more of them than anyone else.

There are eight Pawns.

They are the foot soldiers. Often they must be lost in order to protect the more valuable pieces.

They can also press the attack, inflict crushing losses, and even end the battle by trapping the King!

A Pawn may also be promoted on the field of battle (during a game), much the same as any infantryman today.

The **Castle** is the fort, the refuge, the home. He is easily identified for he looks exactly as he should.

There are two Castles.

The **Knight** is the only professional soldier. (Remember, we said that the chess army was a civilian one.) Incidentally, the term "free lance" comes from this era. It means a Knight who would carry his lance (in other words would fight) for anyone who paid him.

In medieval times people did not travel very much. A man might live a lifetime without going more than thirty miles from his birthplace.

The knights, however, were a different breed of men. They sought adventure, often traveling thousands of miles during the Crusades.

There are two Knights.

This is the **Bishop** who represents the Church.

The Church was very much a part of everyone's life in those days. When we learn how the pieces move we will find how well the Bishop and the Castle work together.

Home and Church—a strong combination! That is as true in life as in the game of chess.

The top of the piece approximates a hat worn by bishops called a miter.

There are two Bishops.

The **Queen** is next. She obviously is woman. And later we'll see that her moves combine both that of the home (Castle) and that of the Church (Bishop). Woman, home, and Church—the most powerful combination on the board!

Perhaps somewhere you've heard the phrase "power behind the throne"? Nowhere is this more true than in the game of chess.

There is but one Queen in chess.

And here is the **King**—royalty—the unquestioned authority, logically too, the tallest piece on the board.

The king was well defended by his subjects, for his capture meant the loss of his kingdom!

This too, is chess. If you do not protect your King you lose the game!

Obviously he is the *most important* (but not the most powerful) piece on the board.

Naturally there is but one King.

Now as we look at a set of chessmen we can imagine them not as meaningless little carvings on a checkerboard but as a complete cross section of the way people lived six hundred years ago, from the most powerful to the very poor.

Part Two

How the Chess Pieces Move

 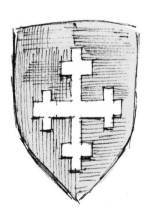 

First let us talk about the chessboard—the battlefield. It looks like this, with thirty-two dark squares and thirty-two light squares.

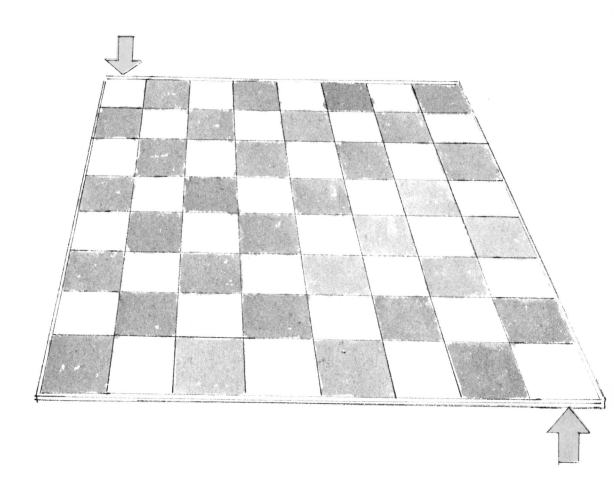

The board cannot be put down casually, but always with a light square in the lower right-hand corner (as you face the board).

The chess pieces move in a number of ways.

One way is *up and down:* dark square to light square to dark to light, etc., towards your opponents' end of the board and back.

Or *from side to side:* dark to light to dark to light, etc.

This is called moving **on the square.**

But there is still another way to move, and that is *from corner to corner.*

This is called moving **on the diagonal.**

On the diagonal move you cross the corner of one square and move into the corner of the next square; you move through squares of the same shade, either light or dark. You may never move through *both* light and dark squares.

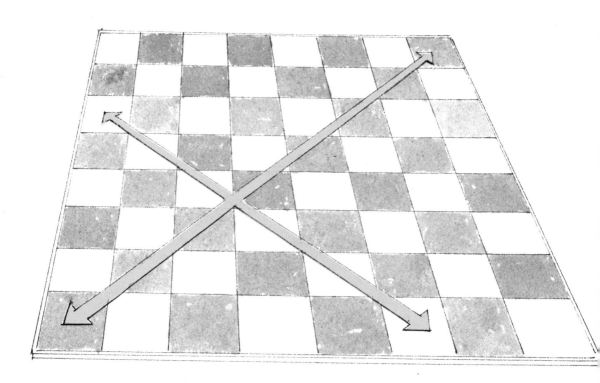

Later, we shall see how different chess pieces use the square and the diagonal to make their moves.

Let's think of the chessboard as a great field of battle, and the chessmen as two armies of equal strength facing each other.

This is the way the pieces are set up at the start of the game.

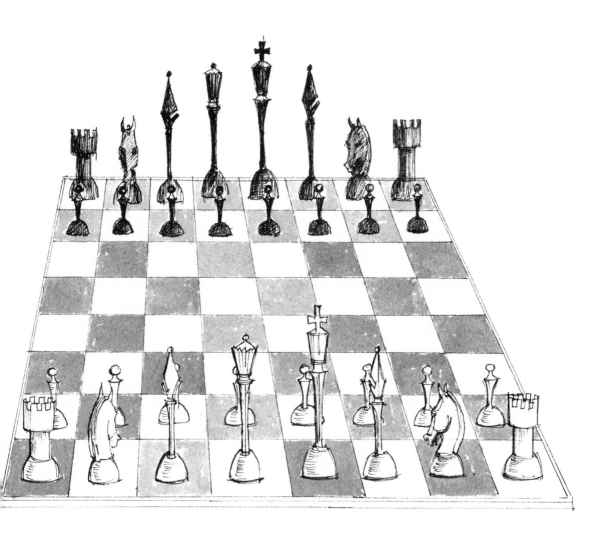

Now we shall set them up, piece by piece.

Across the back of the board (or field of battle, if you like) are placed the more powerful pieces. The fortress-like ones, which are called Castles, are placed in the corners. Like this.

Next to them are the pieces that look like horses. They are the Knights and are placed here.

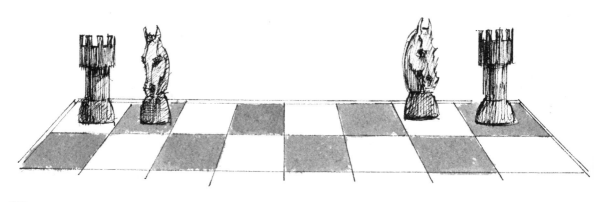

The Church is now represented by the Bishops and are placed so.

In medieval times the Church was next in importance to the rulers (royalty), and in chess too the Bishops' position is an obvious one—next to the King and Queen.

Now there are two empty squares in the center of the board. They are for the King and Queen. But which way do they go? Here we have to remember a little phrase: "Queen on her color." The Black Queen goes on the black square.

Like this.

Now we have placed the important and powerful pieces.

In front of each is placed a Pawn.

They are the foot soldiers, remember? So quite naturally they're in the front lines.

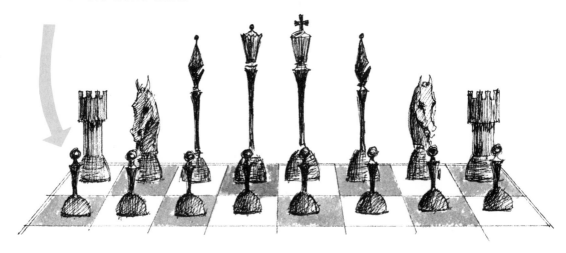

The other side (White) is set up exactly the same. Again with the "Queen on her color." The White Queen on the white square.

White always has the first move. Black is to defend.

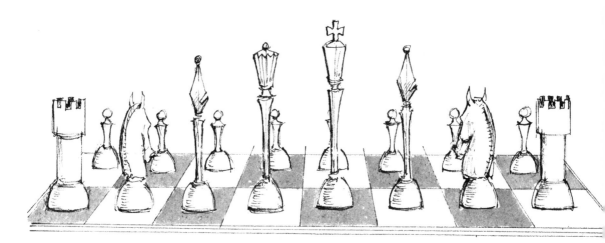

Now let's bring out a chess set, setting the pieces up as we have learned, so we can actually move the pieces!

After all, no matter how much we have read about swimming we have to get wet in order to learn!

The Pawn

Look carefully at the illustration on the facing page, for it explains just how the Pawns move and also how they attack. The way they move and the way they attack are different.)

1. The Pawn *moves one square at a time,* straight ahead.

2. *Pawns may never back up.* And when two enemy Pawns meet in the same row (or file) neither can move.

3. On the first move *only,* each Pawn may move out two squares (if the player wishes). After that, the Pawn may move only one square at a time.

4. Pawns take or capture *only* to the *forward diagonal square, either to the right or left.* Then having removed the enemy piece from the board and taking his place, the Pawn *continues to move straight ahead in the new row. (When moving on the diagonal in capturing,* the Pawn moves across the upper corner of his square and into a square of the same shade as the one he just left.)

Let's see how the chess Pawn looked in actual life. Let us think of Pawns as pikemen. Pikemen were foot soldiers who carried long pikes or spears.

Imagine that they held their shields directly in front of them to protect themselves, and that they held their pikes *pointing to either side.*

Because of his shield he is unable to attack his enemy in the square directly in front of him. He can only attack on the diagonal.

Let us list again some important things to remember about the Pawn.

The Pawn moves one square at a time straight ahead. His attack, however, differs from his move. He *attacks* to the *forward diagonal* square (right or left) and after removing his enemy from the board continues to move straight ahead on his enemy's file.

The Pawn does not seem very powerful, but he can become very important later in the game. If he can fight his way to the opposite end of the board he is promoted—can become any other piece, even a Queen! Of course, never a King. No other chess piece can be promoted to a higher rank. Because they can become powerful, Pawns should be protected by other Pawns or by stronger pieces.

There is also another rule that concerns the Pawn. On the *first* move (and *only* the first move) *each Pawn* has a choice of moving out one or two squares. After that first move he can move only one square at a time.

TO HERE

OR HERE

This unusual first move no doubt reflects the real life situation when the pikemen felt a bit more reckless with his army so close behind him. Later he became cautious and took but one step at a time.

Fighting side by side the pikemen developed a tactic in battle to stop enemy horsemen. They drove the butt end of their pikes into the ground and crouched behind their shields, forming a sort of human pincushion.

Can you imagine what would happen if the Knight should charge?

In the same way our chess Pawns, when properly placed in a game, form a protective wall like the above illustration.

Above is an example of how Pawns back up each other. Let us call them 1, 2, 3, and 4 and place them on the board like this. Remember that the Pawn captures on *the diagonal* (moves diagonally onto a square of the same shade or color).

In our chess battle formation, if Pawn number 3 is attacked, either 2 or 4 can destroy the attacker and move up into the position originally held by 3. In a fight among Pawns there might be a fairly even exchange (Pawn for Pawn), but Pawns are also able to destroy any other piece, and even capture the King himself!

The terms **attack, destroy, capture** all mean the taking of an enemy piece. The word **jump** is a checker term. It is not used in chess.

When you attack you do not jump over an enemy piece. You merely move into the square he occupies and remove him from the board. Your chessman stands exactly where the enemy once stood.

The Castle

Here we see exactly how the Castle *moves and attacks.* (His *attack* does not differ from the *move* as does the pawn).

The Castle moves *up and down,* or *from side to side—*as many squares as he wishes. He can do two things the Pawn cannot. He can move backwards and sideways, but he *cannot* move to the *diagonal.*

As you play chess you will hear the words "rank" and "file." Both are military terms and both are used to explain chess moves.

Rank refers to a row of soldiers, side by side, such as the Pawns at the beginning of a game.

File might be thought of as a single file of soldiers, coming or going.

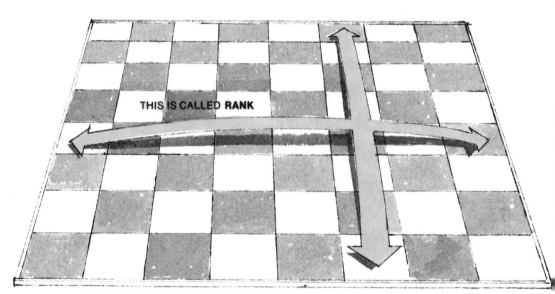

THIS IS CALLED **FILE**

The Castle may sweep across any *open* rank or file.

In the illustration below the Castle may strike any of three Pawns. However one of these attempts would be a most dangerous move.

Do you see which one? and why?

You are the White player.

How would you move your Castle?

The answer is on the following page.

Answer: The Castle might attack either Pawn number 1 or Pawn number 4 and capture them without endangering himself, but if he were to attack Pawn number 2 he himself would be captured by the number 3 Pawn!

Notice how Pawn number 3 backs up Pawn number 2.

The Castle is also known by the name "Rook." In fact, most chess players call it by that name. But to help you remember how it moves we will continue to call it a Castle.

It is easy to think of a castle as being built of great square blocks of stone, with a cornerstone, etc. And logically enough the chess Castles are placed in the corners of the board.

Again, the Castle itself with its huge blocks of stone makes you think of the carpenter and the mason. Their tool, of course, is the square. And that is exactly how this piece moves—*on the square.*

The Castle can attack any enemy piece that is in the **direct path** of his rank or file.

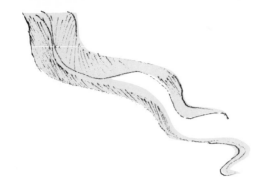

The Knight

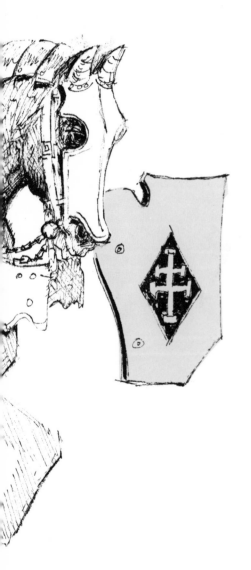

Here is the Knight's move. Notice it is an "L"-shaped move: *two squares in file* (forward or backward) *and then one square in rank* (to either side.)

The Knight can move in any direction, and as you can see from this position has eight possible moves!

The Knight may attack any enemy piece that stands at the end of his move.

His move is a surprising one—a leaping, pivoting, "L"-shaped move—but it can be easily remembered if we think of the actual knight on his charging war horse! We can think of the Knight's move as the jumping of a leaping horse.

Let us imagine that the knight's charge could not be stopped by anyone next to him. Do you think you could stop an armored knight on a trained and spirited horse?

The knight is the *only* chess piece that can jump over another piece, friend or foe.

As we have learned, the knight was the ultimate fighting machine. No foot soldier could withstand his charge, and until the British longbow was introduced the knight was unconquerable.

About the eleventh century a mere seventy knights were able to conquer the entire civilized kingdom of Sicily!

The knight cannot land in a square of the same shade or color as the square from which he jumps.

In the illustration opposite you can see many possible attacks the knight could make.

Do you also see which attacks would be fatal to him?

Answer: The Knight may attack Pawn number 1 or Pawn number 2 without danger to himself.

If he attacks Pawn number 4 or Castle number 5 he himself would be captured on the next move.

Which do you think would be his best move?

Answer: The best move is to attack Castle number 3. Why? In chess, we always try to capture the most powerful pieces first. And the Castle is a more important piece than the Pawn.

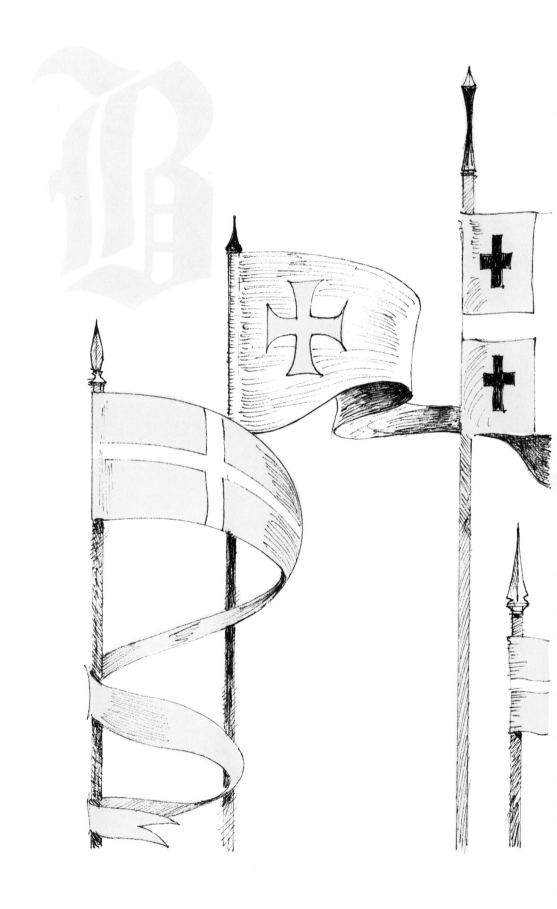

The Bishop

The Bishop moves *on the diagonal* squares, forward or backward as many squares at a time as he wishes.

He may attack any enemy piece that stands on the direct path of his diagonal move.

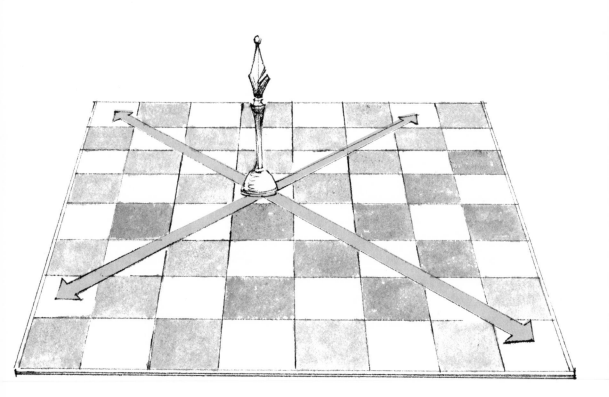

Below is an illustration showing two Bishops at the start of a game.

One Bishop is always on the *dark squares,* the other always on the *light*—throughout the entire game.

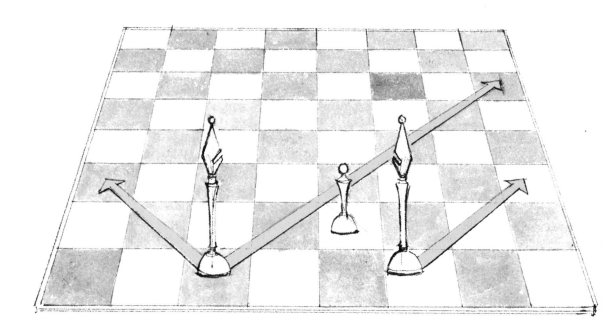

The Bishop on the left has the choice of either diagonal move, since no piece stands in his way. But the Bishop on the right does not have both diagonals open to him. One diagonal is being blocked by one of his own Pawns. The Pawn must be moved to give the Bishop access to that diagonal.

Except for the Knight none of the pieces behind the Pawns can be moved until the Pawns are moved.

Here is an illustration to help you learn the Bishop's move.

In this situation the Bishop has four possible (moves) attacks.

Do you see them? Do you see which attacks would be unwise?

Answer: The Bishop may attack Castle number 1 or Knight number 3, without danger to himself. But were he to attack Pawn number 2 he would be lost to the Knight, and if he attacked Castle number 4 he would be lost to Pawn number 5.

The Queen

In the moves of the Queen we see her tremendous power. Her move combines the power of the Castle with the power of the Bishop!

From this illustration we see she has eight possible directions in which to move and capture!

She can move *forward and backward,* from *side to side,* and *diagonally* as many open squares as she wishes.

She can capture any enemy piece that stands on these avenues of her attack.

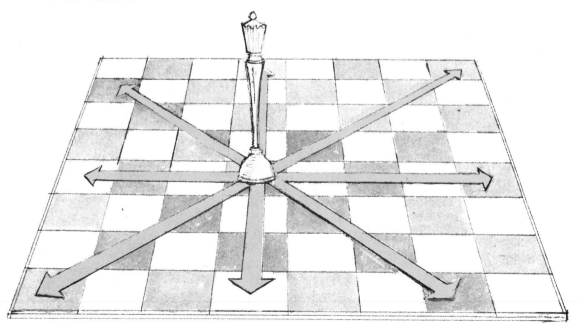

Here we see the Queen among her enemies.

How many pieces do you think she could attack? Count them.

Which of these attacks would result in the Queen's capture?

Answer: The Queen may attack any of the following Black pieces (five in all) without danger of capture:
    either of the Black Bishops, number 5 or 6;
    either of the Black Knights, number 8 or 4.

    Or the Black Castle number 3.

If she attacked number 2 Castle she would in turn be taken by Bishop number 6.

If she attacked Pawn number 1 she would be taken by Knight number 8.

If she attacked Pawn number 7 she would be captured by Castle number 3.

As you can see, it is unwise to attack a piece that is already defended. Always strike the undefended ones!

The King

And at last the ruler, the reason for chess, the King!

His word was law, and his subjects owed their livelihood and allegiance to him. Naturally they would be anxious to see that he survived any battle against an enemy.

So it is in chess. Each piece is moved in an effort to protect their ruler—and capture the enemies.

Notice that the King moves and attacks exactly the same as the Queen, but with kingly deliberation—*only one square at a time.*

On the facing page we see him among his foes.

When the King is threatened with capture we use a term that refers *only* to the King.

This term is the word **check.** It is a warning, and you must say "check" whenever you threaten the enemy King.

When the King is trapped and unable to save himself we say **checkmate** or **check and mate.**

Here is the White King "in check." That is, he would be captured on the next move unless he can avoid it.

Can you see what piece threatens him and what he can do about it?

The Black Knight threatens him.

The White King has but one possible move. Do you see it?

Mark the square (lightly with a pencil) where you think he might go. The answer is on the next page.

A King can get out of check by one of three means. He moves out of the range of the checking piece, he captures the checking piece, or he places one of his men in-between himself and the attached.

Answer: The only possible move for the King is indicated by the arrow.

Obviously in this situation the King's capture is near. When he is finally "checkmated" he surrenders (or rather the player surrenders) like this, and the game is over.

The King is placed down the board—and it's over.

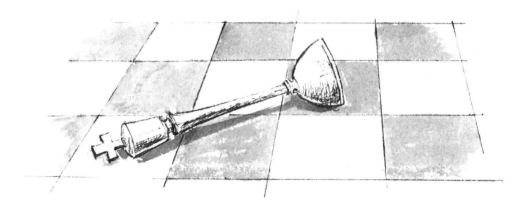

The word "checkmate" comes from the Persian *shah mat* meaning *"the king is dead."*

Later on, when we try to play the game we shall talk more about checking the King.

Castling

Now we are going to talk about a special move that involves the King. Its purpose is to remove the King from possible capture.

This move is called **castling** and is done (only once during a game for each player) with the King and either one of his castles.

The King and the Castle are moved at the same time, as one move.

Castling is simple: move the King two spaces to the side, and then move the *Castle around the King.* This can be done on either side of the King with either Castle.

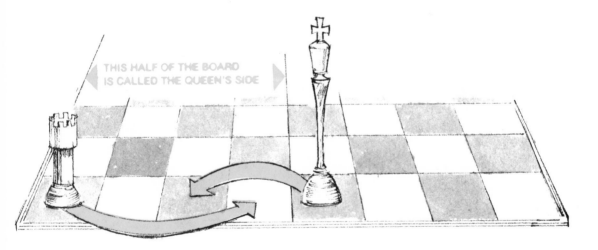

THIS HALF OF THE BOARD
IS CALLED THE QUEEN'S SIDE

This illustration shows how to castle *on the Queen's side.* Only when castling are two pieces moved at the same time.

This is *castling on the King's side.*

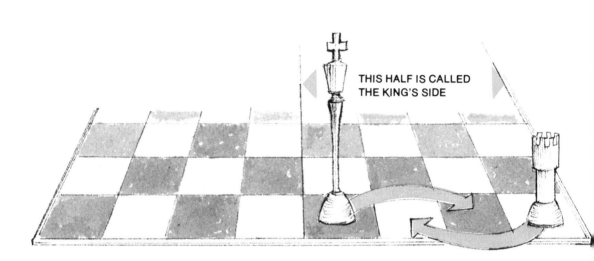

THIS HALF IS CALLED
THE KING'S SIDE

You may castle *only* under these conditions:

1. All the squares between the Castle and King must be open (unoccupied).

2. Only *if* the *King* and the *Castle have not been moved* (since the start of the game).

3. The King may not castle if he is "in check," or if he has to move *through a square threatened* by an enemy piece.

Only once during the game is the King allowed this castling maneuver.

So much for the basic moves of Chess.

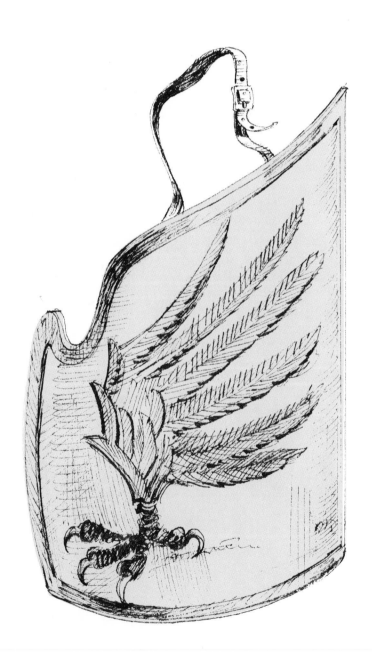

And now we separate the men from the boys.

Part Three

How to Play

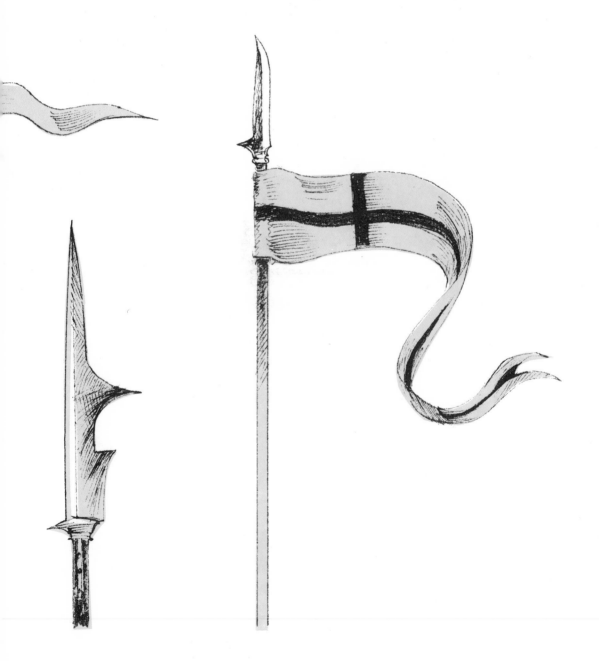

Blitzkrieg: The Quick Game

Now that we are familiar with the pieces and how they move, *let us play an actual game!* You will be the White army.

We are going to have a bit of help with this first game, because we must be sure you understand just what is happening.

We'll call this first game **blitzkrieg.** It comes from the German words *blitz* (meaning "lightning") and *krieg* (meaning "war"), and was a well-known term in World War II.

Literally, "lightning war" was the tactic of striking the enemy at his weakest point with all possible power, making his armies helpless in a very short time.

In the game of chess, White always moves first, but before we begin the game it is well to study the enemy for a moment.

As in any defense there is one weak spot. Chess is no exception to this.

And this pawn is the *one* weakness in Black's defense. Do you see why?

Study the pieces for a moment and you will see that *that particular Pawn* is defended *only* by the *King himself!* (If the Pawn were captured, only the *King himself* could remove the attacker.)

White, too, has a weak spot in its defense, but *because White has the first move* (and consequently the "initiative") *the White army need not be concerned.*

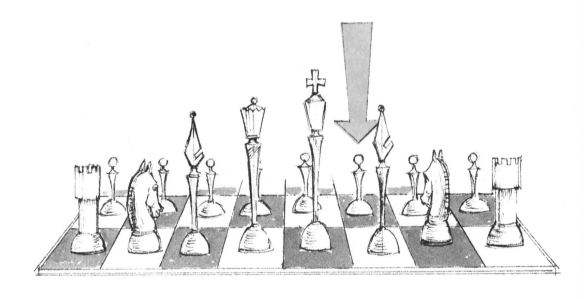

Now we start the game. Remember that we are after the Black King.

We start by moving out with a Pawn (two squares if you like) to the center of the board, like this.

The Pawn is now committed to the battle. And just what does that allow you to do on your *next* move?

The Pawn's move opens up two diagonal avenues. Notice that either the Bishop or the Queen may move to any square on the above dashed lines.

You now have a choice of moving out either of two potentially dangerous pieces!

Black's first move blocks your Pawn with his—a logical and typical countermove.

Now you come out with your Bishop. Do you see that the Bishop now threatens that *one weak Pawn?*

Black again counters by moving his Bishop exactly as the White. It all looks pretty even, doesn't it?

But now, on your move, you bring out your Queen, mounting *more* pressure on that *one weak Pawn*.

Suddenly we enter a critical phase of the battle. As in most battles there is a point where the tide turns and disaster is imminent. Sometimes it is not having enough reserve troops at the needed moment, or merely not recognizing the enemy's strength—or any one of a score of reasons.

But in this game Black simply does not see the threat of your Queen, and comes out with his Knight, like this.

And now you attack with your Queen!

The Black Pawn is taken, and the King is threatened (checked) by the Queen. The King is helpless. He has no place to move to escape the Queen and he cannot capture the Queen for she is "protected" by your Bishop. A King cannot move into a check position.

"Check and mate!" Blitzkrieg in only four moves!

Wasn't that a "lightning" victory? Try this out on a friend, but
watch out in case he knows the blitzkrieg moves too!

How to Begin the Game

Much of the beginner's knowledge is learned the hard way—lose, lose, and lose again.

A few basic rules will help you start the game properly.

1. Try to control the *four center squares* of the board. They get the action, for they are the crossroads of the board.

2. A good first move would therefore be to move the Pawn in front of the King (King's Pawn) two squares.

This not only occupies one of those *four center squares*, but it also opens up diagonal moves for both the Queen and Bishop.

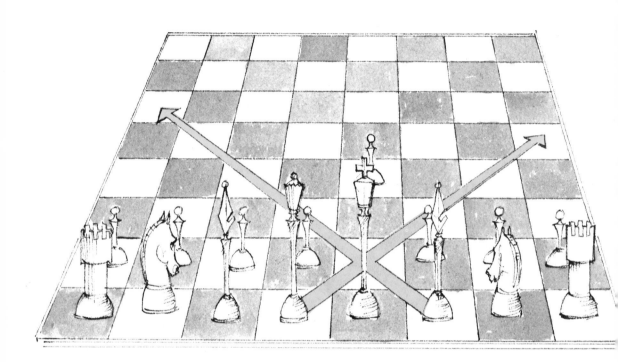

Moving out the Pawn in front of the Queen (Queen's Pawn) is also an acceptable first move.

3. Moving out a Knight is also sound, as long as his next move controls one of those *four center squares*. (See illustration.)

NOT HERE

4. Try to remember to protect (back up) each Pawn as soon as possible (see p. 39).

(Back up each piece you move, for that matter.)

This way of playing weaves a strong defense. You know that none of your men can be taken without an equal loss to the enemy.

A poor opening move would be to move out the Pawn in front of the Knights or Castles. This sort of move does not control or threaten the center of the board. Neither does it open up paths of attack for the Castles.

5. Don't keep moving *the same piece,* unless he is under attack.

If your piece holds or threatens any of those four center squares and he is not in danger, then bring up other pieces to hold more of the center squares.

This is always a sound tactic. *When in doubt as to what to do, bring up more strength:* Pawns, Bishops, Knights, in a slow move toward the opponent's men and King.

Attack and Defense

WHICH ONE WILL BE HIS VICTIM?

Once the game is under way and you have gained control of the center squares, we hope, your next series of moves will be to weaken the enemy's defense of his King. How do you do this?

One way is to open a gap in his defensive line through which we can threaten the King, as in the blitzkrieg game. Another way is to capture as many as possible of your opponent's strong pieces —the Queen, Castle, Bishop or Knight—thereby leaving the King defenseless. If we can capture his Castle, for example, without losing one of our own, we have gained in strength by weakening our opponent's ability to attack us and to defend himself.

As a good general we watch the entire board, looking for enemy pieces that are unprotected—and safe for attack—while at the same time making certain that our own men are safe.

Sometimes in order to gain an advantage in strength we have to give up one of our own men. But in doing so, we'll have a surprise in store for our opponent. Chess is a game of surprises, and the idea is to surprise the enemy, not have him surprise you.

On the facing page we see a knight charging down on two pikemen, and below we have the same situation as represented on the chessboard. Let's pretend that it is your men that are being attacked. What would you do? Watch for surprises!

Because he can be protected, let's say you decide to defend Pawn number 2 by moving up Pawn number 3. Now, it would seem unlikely that the Black Knight would attack Pawn number 2, right? Well, let's see!

Once one of the Pawns is defended the obvious victim is the other Pawn. But supposing the Black Knight decides to withhold his attack and instead brings another piece (a Castle) into the file directly behind him—like this.

Now, when a piece is moved to a certain square you must quickly notice all the directions the piece might go on the next move.

Why do you suppose the Black Castle stopped behind his own Knight when obviously he is being blocked by the Knight? Suppose, though, the Knight moves! Then what is threatened?

You must always notice the entire board and so you follow the possible attack of the Castle and find that in that same file is your Queen!

Still that does not seem to be a particular danger, so you bring up another Pawn to protect Pawn number 1.

Then the Black Knight moves and captures Pawn number 2. It seems like a silly move at first, for now your Queen can easily attack and remove the Black Castle. But can she?

As the Knight captures the Pawn, he also checks (threatens) the King! (Remember you must watch the entire battlefield.)

Now something must be done and quickly! The King must either move out of danger (check), or his attacker must be removed.

If you study this situation for a moment you might say, "What of it if the King is in check? Didn't we 'back up' that Pawn in the first place?" So we'll just take the Black Knight with our Pawn. What an easy victory—a Pawn lost to capture a Knight.

But now the surprise! The Black Castle sweeps down the board to take your unprotected Queen. What a loss!

You must realize that in chess (or warfare) it is not just a matter of a strong defense (or attack). It is also a matter of timing—"when" to attack.

In this case the Black Knight did not strike until his Castle had been brought into position. Then he attacked with two men at once.

Your Pawn was taken although defended, and at the same time your King was checked, the Queen was also threatened by the Castle. And all this happened with one move (of the Knight)!

Of course something had to give! The King had to be saved, and the Queen was lost.

Not the end of the game, to be sure, but nevertheless a crippling blow. Remember that a successful attack must have proper strength, and remember too, WATCH THE ENTIRE BOARD!

Nathan Bedford Forrest, a brilliant Southern general during the Civil War, said of victory in battle that it was merely getting there "fustest with the mostest."

He was a master at striking where he was least expected. As we play chess with more sophistication, we should perhaps keep his famous phrase in mind: "fustest with the mostest."

Blitzkrieg Revisited

Now we have played a complete game and we've learned a bit about how to begin the game (those all-important *four center squares*). We've learned a little more about attack and defense. So now let's play another game, and see what we've learned.

You've seen how quickly a game can be won. So now you try the old blitz game again. Why not?

This time, however, we'll pretend that you're playing with someone with more experience.

You begin (White) and find that each of your moves is met with the same defense until the game resembles exactly the game on page 87.

This now becomes exciting and you wait expectantly for Black to fall into the same fatal trap!

Will it happen? Let's see.

Black, however, comes out with his *other* Knight (note, page 88), blocking your Queen's threat! Now what to do?

It seems obvious now that your Queen's attack has been stopped, and after some thought you decide to bring out a Pawn to back up your Bishop and Pawn (a cautious move).

Black, too, seems to be cautious as he moves out a Pawn.

Not knowing what to do, you then make another cautious Pawn move. At this point something you can't see has passed from you to your opponent. It is called "initiative."

You kept the initiative during the entire previous game—and won, because at all times you knew just what you wanted to do.

Here you're uncertain, and as soon as your enemy sees this, watch out!

No doubt you know what it is like to walk through a swamp or bog. You can't move very fast, can you?

And when this happens to an attack in battle (literally, when the attack "bogs down") it is an ideal time for your enemy to strike!

After your second indecisive move Black strikes—a **Counterattack!**

Black moves out two squares with a Pawn, simultaneously threatening *both your Pawn and your Bishop!* (A move like this which
threatens two pieces is called a fork.) Note too, that the Pawn is
defended three ways (Pawn, Knight, and Queen)!

The Bishop cannot escape, so the Black Pawn *must* be removed.

Obviously the best way to dispose of that troublesome Black Pawn is to take him with your Pawn, as shown above, and await Black's next counter.

Notice that although you have removed one of Black's men (the Pawn) you no longer have the initiative. You're waiting to see what the enemy is planning.

And of course the more sophisticated your opponent, the less likely you will be able to anticipate his strategy.

Exchanging Pawns would keep the balance of power, but if we could lose a Pawn to capture a Knight or Bishop—without endangering our position—we would be ahead in strength and power.

Here *Black* (the experienced player) *does the unexpected.* Instead of taking your Pawn with his he opens up an entirely new area of the battle, threatening your Queen with his Bishop! Your Queen has but one safe square in which to move! Each of the other squares is controlled by a black piece and the threatening Bishop is protected by a Knight.

There is no other alternative. Your Queen *must move to this position!*

The pressure is obviously on you, and without lessening it Black now removes his King to a safer position and at the same time brings another strong piece into play.

This is done by castling, as shown.

You're still a bit worried about your Queen, and would like very much to extricate her. And there it is—you spot an undefended Pawn.

This probably is your most serious mistake since your blitz attack bogged down. For Black merely moves his Castle into your Queen's file!

Now you're in real trouble, for your Queen cannot escape without exposing your King! (And then the game is over!) So you're forced to take the Black Castle.

As you take the Black Castle you also check the Black King! But this moment of glory may be short-lived.

Notice that you've captured *three* Black pieces against *no losses.*

The Black Queen captures the White Queen, and puts your King in check.

Your King must either *be moved out of check, or the threat must be blocked.* You have several choices. But remember: a *wrong decision* in chess (or in battle) *may be fatal.* Usually you're not lucky enough to have a second chance.

For example: suppose you decide to protect your King by blocking the threat with your Knight.

Do you think this is an adequate defense? Let's see.

Unfortunately it is not, for the Black Queen's attack is backed up by her Bishop!

"Check and mate" and it is over!

Notice that once the counterattack had begun (p. 106) Black never let up the pressure, continually harassing and crowding, so that the strong White pieces could not be used for anything but the defense of the King. And then came the fatal mistake, and it's over!

As an exercise, return to page 114, setting up the board exactly as it was at the time of the Black Queen's check.

This time, however, block the Queen's check with your Bishop (rather than the Knight) and from this see how well you can defend and prolong the battle.

This was a much longer game than your blitz attack (p. 83) and you lost too! But nevertheless it was fun, and you have learned a few surprising tactics.

It's always helpful to analyze our mistakes, regardless. But remember in chess mistakes really hurt!

How to End the Game

To end the game the enemy King must be put in check (threatened, in other words) by one of your pieces and be unable to get out of it.

Here are some thoughts about how you can accomplish this.

1. *Study the King's position,* and look for that key square. A **key** square is the one weak spot in the King's defense. (Sometimes there is more than one key square).

The key square in this case would be the square occupied by this Pawn. Do you see why?

Answer: all the other pieces are protected (or do not involve the King's defense). *This particular Pawn* is protected only by the *King.*

If the Black pieces were arranged like this, this would be the key square for White to occupy.

Here the Black King is trapped by his own men. (They are in his way, and he has no escape.)

Here the key square is also unprotected, so if a White Queen or Castle could move into that square it would have to be "check and mate."

2. Once you have decided where the key square is, *zero in* on it—with all possible strength.

The key square is not always *near the King* (as in the above illustration). Consequently your opponent does not see the danger to his King until it is too late.

3. It is usually best to put your *most powerful* piece into that key square (preferably your Queen).

4. Be sure, however, that the key square is properly backed up before you attack! That square can be backed up by several pieces—the more the better, for sometimes the check does not hold. (Your opponent is able to escape.) The more power that can be brought to bear on a *key area,* the quicker the game will be over.

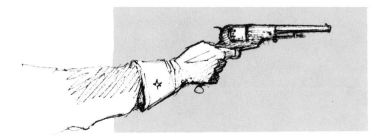

This finding of the key square comes gradually. It comes with being *thoroughly familiar* with the way each piece moves.

Right now it is not too easy to see it. However, as you play more and more chess you'll find it becomes easier and easier. It is also excellent training if you really want to master the game.

There are many ways of ending the game. Sometimes your opponent falls into something stupid—a careless mistake—and you must be quick to take full advantage of his error. (Again, this comes from being *thoroughly familiar* with the way each piece moves.) Remember there is no luck and no mercy in chess.

To repeat: The best way to end the game (after the first few opening moves) is to

1. Study the King's position on the board.

2. Decide which is the key square.

3. Begin to bring pressure on that area with several pieces. This pressure (and counterpressure by the enemy) builds up slowly. It is usually spoken of as the "middle" game in chess.

4. Finally, attack that key square! Attack it with your most powerful piece (your Queen if possible).

5. Once the attack is started, keep the King in check with every move, until finally there is no place for him to hide, and it's over. "Check and Mate!"

Some Random Thoughts

Now you have learned the game of chess. To be sure, you're not a great player, but how many "push-ups" did you do the first time? or how well did you swim a year ago? or bat a ball? It all has to be developed. And it is the same with chess.

But now that you learned the game you should feel a great sense of accomplishment, *and be proud of yourself!*

For not everyone can play. Some become confused or bored (depending on their temperaments) or "go to pieces." It is exciting, isn't it, when the attack builds or the defense is exasperatingly firm?

You can play and enjoy chess all your life. (It's like swimming— you never forget how). And you can play with *anyone,* grownups most of all. (It is fun when you beat them!)

You've also learned an international language, for chess is played almost everywhere in the world.

Come on—I'll play you!